Straight from the Heart

Straight from the Heart
Our World in Poetry

JOHN MORGAN MULLEN

Copyright © 2022, John Morgan Mullen

All rights reserved. Printed in the U.S.A.

No part of this publication may be reproduced or transmitted in any form or by any means, electronic or mechanical, including photocopy, recording or any information storage and retrieval system now known or to be invented, without permission in writing from the publisher, except by a reviewer who wishes to quote brief passages in connection with a review written for inclusion in a magazine, newspaper or broadcast.

Quantity Purchases:
Companies, professional groups, clubs, and other organizations may qualify for special terms when ordering quantities of this title.
For information, email info@ebooks2go. net,
or call (847) 598-1150 ext. 4141.
www.ebooks2go.net

Published in the United States by eBooks2go, Inc.
1827 Walden Office Square, Suite 260, Schaumburg, IL 60173

ISBN: 978-1-5457-5564-8 (Paperback)
ISBN: 978-1-5457-5572-3 (Hardcover)

Library of Congress Cataloging in Publication

Contents

Introduction xi

CHAPTER ONE: LIFE

1. Today is Yesterday's Tomorrow 3
2. We made it Thru the Rain 4
3. Character. 5
4. We Only Get One Life 6
5. Fear 7
6. Mentoring is a Two Way Street 8
7. Cancer Fear 9
8. Education vs Experience 10
9. Anxiety, Depression & Hope 11
10. Cancer Sucks! 12
11. Intelligence, Wisdom & Brilliance 13
12. Money 14
13. I Hope You Dance 15
14. Let's Go Home 16
15. Success is Not a Straight Line 17
16. Fear is My Friend 18
17. Meeting with Myself 19
18. Game Plan 20
19. Coronavirus 21
20. Our World 23
21. My Two Worlds 24

22. Michigan Home 25
23. Risk & Fear. 26
24. Please God 27
25. Heaven's Team 28
26. SetBacks are Hard 29
27. Nothing is Easy. 30
28. Respect. 31

CHAPTER TWO: DREAMS, HOPE & LOVE

1. Hope. 35
2. Is It Half Empty or Half Full? 36
3. The Day the Hope Died. 37
4. Power of WE 38
5. Hope and Love 39
6. I Promise... 40
7. The Power of Thoughts. 41
8. Dream World. 42
9. I Believe I Can Fly 43
10. Sex 44
11. I Remember... 45
12. What is Love? 47
13. You Had Me at "Hello" 49
14. One Step at a Time. 50
15. Courage of Change. 51
16. Change or Die 52
17. Grandson & Friend. 53
18. "It's a Girl". 54
19 The Mansard Friends. 55

20. The Men of Sparta	56
21. Kids & Kids Kids	57
22. Fishing is more than Fish	58
23. Fly Away	59
24. A Dreamer's Promise	60
25. My Dream For Us	61

CHAPTER THREE: POLITICS

1. Decisions	65
2. I Believe	66
3. Political Choices	67
4. I Have a Dream	69
5. Political Leaders	71
6. Government Stinks	72
7. Middle East	73
8. Patriotic American	75
9. Dear Politician, I'm Sorry	76
10. War	78

CHAPTER FOUR: SPECIAL OCCASION

1. Happy "I Do"	81
2. Anniversary Number Forty-nine	82
3. Happy Anniversary (2014)	83
4. Happy Anniversary-#53	84
5. Anniversary Love	86
6. Birthday Formula	87
7. New Year's Dreams	88

8.	Special Christmas Gift	89
9.	Another Birthday…Another Year	90
10.	Dear Jill, It's Hard to Say Goodbye	91
11.	Christmas is But Once a Year	92
12.	Happy Birthday Wish	93
13.	Dear Mom	94
13.	MSU 50 Years	95
14.	Lowell's Dash	96
15.	Merry Christmas Gifts	97
16.	Happy Birthday & Happy Mother's Day	98
17.	Happy Valentine's Day True Love	100
18.	Happy 50th Anniversary	101
19.	Christma's Love	102
20.	It's MY TIME	103
21.	Dreamer's Promise	104
22.	Please Say "YES"	105
23.	Gift of Love	106
24.	Love Grows with Time	107
25.	The Power of ME	108

CHAPTER FIVE: THE FINAL CHAPTER

1.	The Winter of Our Life	111
2.	Our Retirement World	113
3.	Road Map to Tomorrow	114
4.	Getting Old	115
5.	Retirement for a Guy like Me	116
6.	How Old is Old?	117

7. Closer to the Unknown. 118
8. Beyond Life & Death 119
9. Illusions & Dreams 120
10. Ok….What's Next. 121
11. After the Game. 122
12. Our Strength is in our Body & Mind 123
13. Family 124
14. The Love of My Life .125
15. The Push. 126
16. Those Left Behind 127
17. The Day Grief Dies. .128
18. "Jill"…Jill…Are You There?". 129
19. Love 130
20. Great Ride 131
21. The Power Within 132
22. A Great Love Affair. .133
23. Beautiful Memories. 134
24. Yesterday, Today & Tomorrow (Past, Present & Future) . . .135
25. Love Story 136
26. Change. 137
27. Love is Forever. 138
28. Dear God. 139
29. Is the Game Over? .140
30. Myself 141
31. Alone. 142

Note from the Author 143

Introduction

"Straight from the Heart", evolved from years of expressing my feeling in the form of poetry. It started in lieu of greeting cards and expanded as a way to express my inner feelings on almost any subject. Poetry allows and even requires the poet to crawl inside his soul in describing and presenting his thoughts through his poems.

This book is dedicated to my wife, Jill as it depicts our life thru poetry. It outlines ventures and journey that we have taken, side by side. Our lives have ventured thru good and bad, through the joys and excitement that life has presented and those special moments throughout of lives that can never be replace.

My poems are directed to our everyday life's issues of Love and Dreams, Courage and Fears, Character and Inspirations and even Politics. Many of the Poems presented required and include some personal experiences with a peek inside our personal lives.

Within the collection of poems you will find that some are serious, some include humor and all, hopefully are enlightening and entertaining. I talk about Hope and Fear as well as Sickness and Death. These poems talk about "The Guy in the Mirror", "Respect", and "I Made it Thru the Rain". I talk about "The Power of WE", "Mentoring is a Two Way Street" and how "Success is Not a Straight Line."

Our road has not always been easy, but our love has always remained strong. These words are especially dear to my heart as Cancer has raised its ugly head and my wife will be reading these beautiful poems from heaven.

My poems talk about our inspirational life's lessons that are found throughout our lives for the past 55 years. Love truly does conquer all.

John Morgan Mullen

Chapter One
Life

Today is Yesterday's Tomorrow

We struggle with our reflections of yesterday.
But we can't change yesterday today.
So yesterday's pain remains our sorrow.
Because today is yesterday's tomorrow.

Maybe we can rewrite our pain.
And maybe we can break the futures chain.
But yesterday is not ours to borrow.
Because today will always be yesterday tomorrow.

Now tomorrow is ours to create.
And today is the difference we can make.
So let not worry about yesterday.
Let's love and be happy today and tomorrow.

Our reflections of yesterday will never change.
But today and tomorrow we can rearrange.
Happiness is built on our today and tomorrow.
But today will always be yesterday's tomorrow.

John Morgan Mullen

We Made It Thru the Rain

Sometimes life is like our very own thunder storm.
It's unpredictable, violent with destruction beyond the norm.
Everything from death, heartaches, financial collapse and pain.
Creating fears that you can never, "Make it Thru the Rain".

Life's hard knock are a two way street.
They tear us apart as we learn from our defeats.
Life's lessons will never have been in vain.
As they help us "Make it thru the Rain".

We negotiate life's roadblocks every day,
To chase the fears of storms away.
To search and reach beyond the clouds,
Find greatness and rise above the crowds.

Barry Manilow's song provides beautiful insight.
Into our complicated world with foresight.
We grow with adversity as well as our success.
We learn from our victories as well as our stress.

If dreamers were to have their way,
The sun will chase away the rain everyday.
While it washes away our innocent's and pain,
In order for us to "Make it Thru the Rain."

John Morgan Mullen

Character

Character is acquired from life's' lessons we've learned.
They are mental and moral hard knocks we righteously earned.
Character is when you pick yourself up and get back into the game.
Realizing that we don't win 'em all and accept the blame.

Success is never achieved without mistakes along the way.
As we realize life is full of detours with tolls we must pay.
Our character is our moral compass & who we are.
The good, the bad & sometimes even a shining star.

Character is not a gift and it must be learned.
It must be cherished, respected and earned.
Character is powerful, character is the lessons of our youth.
Character is hard with the ultimate character found in truth.

John Morgan Mullen

We Only Get One Life

When young we freely venture into our world with
ambition and hope.
As the dials on our clock move faster until we're at the
end of my rope.
The day before yesterday, we were trying to figure out what to do.
And now our time has passed as we get older
and we're almost through.

While our accomplishments were many so were our mistakes.
They filled our hearts with joy but also made our heart ache.
We don't always get "do overs" like we did in school.
We own our yesterday's which is good but sometimes cruel.

Kids and Grandkids makes us grin and smile.
They challenge us and make our journey worthwhile.
As we venture into our world of the "chip off the old block".
Creating duplicate copies as we attempt to improve our future stock.

We progress with a reoccurring merry-go-round for our creations,
With hope that our lesson will filter thru to our future generation.
As we try our best to improve our world and manage our stress,
As we search for perfection with a little hope of success.

John Morgan Mullen

Fear

Fear is an emotion that only you can give it the fuel to exist.
A feeling of shivering terror that cannot be easily dismissed.
It can generate incredible power from deep within your soul,
That can control your universe and puts your life on hold.

Change is a major factor on what fears is based.
Change is new unfamiliar territory that needs to be faced.
As we look fear in the face we realize it can be overthrown
And the more fear is faced the more it can be dethroned.

While fear can be healthy, you must certainly control.
For success to be accomplished and achieve your goal.
So keep your fear close but don't back down.
Unless your research dictates your plan is not sound.

Fear requires diligence preparation and care
To eliminate mistakes, carelessness, wear and tear.
Interestingly fear can also be our friend.
It eliminates the risk of throwing caution to the wind.

Courage and determination are the weapons to clear
Freedom is generated by the elimination of fear.
Eliminating fear provides the courage & wisdom we lack.
Controlling fear will put you back on the right track.

John Morgan Mullen

Mentoring is a Two Way Street

Successful Mentoring is a two way street.
It's stimulating when education and experience meet.
Information sharing benefits everything we see.
The power of "I" is compounded by the knowledge of "we".

A Mentor is a teacher with experience to share.
This donation of knowledge, patience and care.
An ambitious student with talent works best.
To achieve great results and surpass the rest.

When information and experience becomes a team,
They can accomplish anything as they achieve the dream.
The Mentor contributes lessons both good and bad
And knowledge from his world and skills he's had.

As the Mentored develops and they achieve great things.
They believe they can fly as they spread their wings.
It started with "I" and progressed to "we"
And those that I've mentored now mentor me.

John Morgan Mullen

Cancer Fear

Cancer strikes fear in our heart.
It slaps us in the face and tears us apart.

As we are struggling trying to be remain strong.
But it doesn't care because it dances to its own song.

Cancer could care less if you are young or old.
It becomes part of your body as it penetrates your soul.

We are searching everywhere trying to find hope,
As we are rapidly getting close to the end of our rope.

The doctors and their medicine are getting closer everyday
To finding a cure but it is still miles away.

It's inside our body and it and has a mind of its own.
While we may have strong support, we are still all alone.

So our fear is multiplied as we get closer to the end.
It's a race to the finish that we are trying to win.

John Morgan Mullen

Education vs Experience

What's more important "Education" or "Experience"?
Both require diligence, hard work and perseverance.

We can never duplicate the experiences we achieved.
Including the added value of the education received.

Education trains the mind as to how to think.
Knowledge and Experience are both interlinked.

Education expands the mind without a doubt.
But experience teaches us what to think about.

We strive for a balance of personal and professional growth
So is it Education or Experience?....the answer is BOTH!

John Morgan Mullen

Anxiety, Depression & Hope

Anxiety is an internal disease that originates in the mind
and destroys hope.

It creates a sense of apprehension that eliminates our capacity to cope.

It generates tremendous pressure from peers that initiate
fear and rejection,

With our minds being filled with self-doubt due to our imperfection.

This disease is accompanied by anger, hostility, hopelessness
and a depressive state.

If left untreated it can spiral out of control with death
as a possible fate.

Our younger generations are the first to be mentally
attacked & terrorized.

Anxiety and depression are real and scary and more
abundant than ever realized.

Research is beginning to allow us to understand the
problem we must face,

And the hurdles of more and more lives of our fallen
angels in this death race.

Please help spread your love, our mutual hope
and your contributions for sure,

As we need help to utilize all our strength and compassion
as we try to find a cure.

John Morgan Mullen

Cancer Sucks!

Cancer strikes fear in our heart.
We try to be brave but it tears us apart.
We pray hard that the doctors are wrong.
It boggles our mind and we need to be strong.

We fall to our knees when given the news.
It's a stab in the heart in a game most lose.
With dedication and hard work, a solution we will secure.
As the best medical minds are getting closer to a cure.

We need to stay strong in our medical belief.
That the discoveries of tomorrow will bring us relief.
With our knowledge and technology being increased.
We are prepared to defeat this horrible beast.

With Medical technology we are committed to fight.
"Why Me" we continually ask both day and night.
Life give us both good and bad luck,
But having Cancer really sucks!

John Morgan Mullen

Intelligence, Wisdom & Brilliance

To have intelligence only gets you part of the way
As Wisdom trumps intelligence every minute of every day

Being smart might give us the answers to the questions we ask
But Wisdom & brilliance helps us to understand and solve them fast

Wisdom & Brilliance is more than just knowledge but encompasses critical thinking as well
They determine when to hold 'em and when to fold 'em or when to buy and when to sell

Ideally, we solve our issues utilizing Wisdom, intelligence and brilliance in equal shares
Intelligence provides knowledge, brilliance finds solutions and wisdom evaluates what's fare

Intelligence is learned, Wisdom is experience, but Brilliance is a dream come true
It's rare to possess all three so we attempt to do the best we can do

We strive for perfection as we prepare to turn life's page
With intelligence, brilliance and wisdom the world becomes our stage

John Morgan Mullen

Money

No pension, no trust fund, no silver or gold,
No retirement nest egg, annuity for when I get old.

Interest in real estate is not always a good bet.
It's has its up and down and of course there's the debt.

I enjoyed my work and continue today.
A deal here and there if comes my way.

I don't seem to need much but Jill might disagree.
We enjoy life's' comforts but money remains the key.

I like money, it's useful and better to have it than not.
There were times I had very little and times I had a lot.

I always want more but it becomes harder to get.
It requires effort and risk without a safety net.

Money has no friendships, loyalty or love.
No borders, no faith nor help from above.

Try and not get attached because it will eat you alive.
It's comes and it goes but we need it to survive.

John Morgan Mullen

I Hope You Dance

You grow up in a world filled with hopes and dreams.
And we want the best life has to give, as it is not always what it seems.
And when life gives you the chance to sit it out or dance,
We pray you give life a fighting chance and hope you chose to dance.

You can stay on the sideline and never venture onto the world stage.
Play it safe, and never risk failure but you will always
stay on the same page
Or you can experience the joys and the risks life has in store,
And magnify the success, the thrills, the sorrows and much more.

Hopefully love will never leave you empty handed,
As the risk of love is filled with a fear of being stranded.
May you always cherish that sense of wonder,
With that magical anticipation life has you under.

Take that leap of faith and through caution to the wind,
And commit to love and start playing to win.
You can't be happy if you don't give life a chance,
And when given the chance I hope you choose to dance.

John Morgan Mullen

Let's Go Home

In our lives we have ventured both near and far.
We've spent our time chasing that shining star.
Michigan, Utah and Chicago we freely roam.
We have loved every minute but now it's time to go home.

Our roots are in Chicago along with our hearts.
Let's pack up our memories and head back to the start.
The most important things in our world will be just down the street,
Allowing us to play, help, hug, love and meet.

These will be the last holidays we will spend alone.
As we rebuild our world within our family zone.
This is what is right for us and we need to do.
This is the answer to our prayers for me and you.

Our present to each other is located on Dobson Lane.
It's time to reunite, rejoice and breakout the Champaign.
Our travels and experiences were enhanced as we roam,
But now is the time pack up car and Lets Go Home.

John Morgan Mullen

Success is Not a Straight Line

Your world is full of hopes and dreams.
Nothing is what it first seems.

Persistence is the key to achieving success.
Greatness is realized as you progress.

Some say intelligence, and others say megabucks.
Some say breaks, and some say just luck.

No one succeeds without mistakes,
Without pain and suffering and heartaches.

If the pot of gold is to be redeemed,
Persistence holds the key to achieving your dreams.

Our road to happiness we strive to find,
And we realize that success is not a straight line.

John Morgan Mullen

Fear Is My Friend

Fear is scary and gets your attention fast.
If not faced head on, it will forever last.

Fear of failure is your worst nightmare,
And the courage to fight is your dare.

Battle your fear, as it is a destroyer of dreams.
Conquer your fear with actions that redeem.

Fear is a great motivator in many ways.
With time and hard work, dividends it pays.

Knowledge and preparation combat your fears.
Face each of them head on as they appear.

If mistakes and corrections are needed to mend,
Listen and remember as…fear is my friend.

John Morgan Mullen

Meeting with Myself

Periodic meetings to know where you are at,
To confirm the right road and direct your internal chat.
Between insanity and brilliance is a fine line.
Both require thinking outside the box and in your mind.

It refreshes your direction and defines your role.
It brightens your objectives and describes your soul.
Agendas work best so that you don't lose track,
To point out where you want to go and what you lack.

There are many areas of expertise within your mind.
This knowledge is called upon many, many times.
Maybe it's legal or financial, or maybe the creative girl or guy.
They are all present and continually question, "Why?"

You are compromised by the inner voices in your head.
You listen and learn by what is said
During the private conversations among your many selves
As they discuss your options to determine what sells.

Sometimes you need decisions and sometimes not.
Each has his or her opinion, and sometimes things get hot.
As you continue to evaluate and strive to impress,
Your Meetings with Myself will increase your success.

John Morgan Mullen

Game Plan

A wish is a goal without a plan.
Review often to determine where you stand.

Write it down and check it twice.
Success depends on it, so be concise.

A plan provides the road to your dreams.
Follow the path and determine what it means.

When personal and professional goals are attained.
Congratulations as your imagination is now unchained.

Hard work and commitment go hand and hand.
Success is determined by following your game plan.

John Morgan Mullen

Coronavirus

Normally, Christmas time is the best time of the year.
It brings us joy being close to family and all that is dear.
But the virus is overtaking our world and affecting our family fun,
Curtailing the celebrations within our family until Covid-19 is done

We handle the adversity and loneliness as best we can,
As we all fight the Coronavirus' challenges throughout the land.
Knowing we are a communal world that requires that personal touch
And are forced to eliminate that which we miss so very much.

Be it holidays or birthdays celebrations with friends that we toast,
We require those gentle moments together with those
that matter the most.
Our personal and emotional health is considered at high risk.
If not fed, thru contact and love, its joys will be dearly missed.

So let's take the vaccine step and pray that it will do the trick,
Our emotional and financial world depends on it and hopefully quick.
Maybe this worldwide tragedy will bring the nations
of our world together
Fighting this common enemy allowing us to mend our difference forever.

We are frontline soldiers & will fight the Coronavirus until we win.
We care less what company provides the vaccine but rather when.
We want to get back to our lives, hopefully in one piece,
as quick as we can.
Stop this disaster and get back to where we started before this began.

We're tired of this isolation and need the emotional love
and support we miss.

We are the warriors of this WAR that long for that hug
and especially that kiss.

Our family is stronger than this virus & we want our life back
but can't do it alone.

We need to put this isolation behind us & return to our Family
& Friends zone.

John Morgan Mullen

Our World

When young we venture into our world with life to master
But with each day the dials on our clock move faster and faster
The day before yesterday in college, we were trying
to figure out what to do
And now our time has passed and we're almost through

While our accomplishments were many so were our mistakes
They filled our hearts with joy and also made our hearts ache
We don't always get "do overs" like we did in school
We own our yesterdays whether right, wrong, kind or cruel

Kids and Grandkids makes us grin and smile
They challenge us and make our journey worthwhile
As we venture into our world of the "chip off the old block"
Creating duplicate copies as we attempt to improve our future stock

We progress with a reoccurring merry-go-round for each generation
With hope that our lesson will filter thru bringing
personal gratification
We try our best to improve our world as we clean up our mess
We search for the impossible perfection with little hope of success

John Morgan Mullen

My Two Worlds

Chicago is great and I love the City
It's exciting, it's fun but the traffic is a pity
It's work, it's crowds, business and pleasures
It's family and friends, with all their treasures

Its competitive, it's ruthless, it's relationship loaded
It's challenging, it's political and the crime is well noted
Four days a week I am able to get my fix
And return to heaven every weekend for my kicks

Michigan is the opposite of my hectic city life
It's slower, peaceful and lazy without the strife
It's golf, fishing, swimming and grandkid fun
It rejuvenates my soul as I play in the sun

We all need our heaven and this is mine
For peace and quiet as I wet my line
Both of my worlds are great but worlds apart
I love 'em both as they are my piece of my art.

John Morgan Mullen

Michigan Home

Michigan is where I make my home
It's slower, It's peaceful it's my comfortable zone

Hunters and fisherman as they catch fish and shoots deer
It's family and fun, throughout the year

Retired baby boomers, Auto industry people everywhere
Just normal people where crime is very rare

Golf, fishing, hunting, boating and more
Friendly, compassionate, both rich and poor

Not like the Big City, which I liked a lot
But peaceful, serene and hectic it's not

South for the winter is an annual affair
Mexico, Florida, Arizona they don't care

There are more deer than people that's a fact
More pick-up than cars but traffic we lack

I like the sun in the morning rising as I awake
The moon and the stars at night reflecting over the lake

I miss the City, but no longer do I roam
As Michigan is where I make my home.

John Morgan Mullen

Risk & Fear

Risk & Fear are abundant at seventy-five
By most standards, it's amazing I'm still alive
Our world is filled with joyful and tragic events
Providing Life's highs and low that are sometimes intense

The results of Risk are part of life's game
But without risk our lives would never be the same
Risk is often your enemy but sometime it's your friend
We let our fear rule as we think that the risk may win

Many elect not to play for fear of looking like a fool
But dreams will never be achieved without the risk of not being cool
Self-courage is essential when fighting to survive
To succeed you must be commit to focus and drive

Risk & fear are necessary combination if we want to succeed
They feed on one another are two emotions we desperately need
Like the risk of love is full of excitement but also fear
Sometime it's difficult to find happiness without a few tears

We have but one shot at our world where we live
It doesn't come with second chances that we take or we give
So if we want play life's game, it comes abundantly clear
We need to face our demons and learn to live with Risk & Fear

John Morgan Mullen

Please God

Please God heal our daughter and her family's pain
Brennan's loss fills our hearts with tears like rain

How do we find comfort, how do we cope?
How do we regain ANY sense of hope?

Our days are filled with a chain of endless hurt and fears
Please help us thru our pain as we share our mutual tears

Our world has been devastated and changed forever.
Oh God please give us a sign so we might all heal together.

John Morgan Mullen

Heaven's Team

Heaven's a great place to start reassembling our Team.
Maybe the bond we established was more than just a dream.

You've already got Bubba, George, Thornhill, Wedemeyer, & Kenny,
And Cotton, Conti, Heft & Richardson and the forgotten many.

Check and see if you can find Duffy, he's gottta be up there.
Probably already coaching the Angels or the Saints somewhere.

OK, so maybe we're a little out of shape.
But we'll have access to miracles and a lot of tape.

So talk to God, as it could be our last shot at Fame.
Hopefully we will qualify and be drafted at the end of our game.

We will all be humming the Spartan Fight Song tune.
Your friends and family will miss you and be joining you soon.

John Morgan Mullen "15"

Setbacks are Hard

To combat setbacks, we keep swinging and continue to try;
Though at times we are devastated and we wonder why.

Patience and hard work we hope will pay;
As we continue our journey day by day.

When you lose big it's hard to recover.
We are ostracized and our friends we soon discover.

Losers are lonely as we all like winners
We find our true self as we revert back to beginners

Nobody likes to start over at any age
Especially when turning over your last page

My strength is being tested to see if I pass
To see how I react after losing my ass

Our challenges help to keep us humble
Success is impossible without a stumble

Winning is fun...loosing is not
Just don't give up when thing get hot

Set backs are stepping stones across the stream
They show us the way, as nothing is as it seems

John Morgan Mullen

Nothing is Easy

It doesn't make any difference if it money or love
The picture changes with each step or shove

Life's battles are always filled with hurdles that surprise
Evaluate your objective and think compromise

We muddle thru our problems as they come our way
So plan as best you can and make adjustment each day

Some are insurmountable and some we learn to master
Whether it be progress, success, triumph or disaster

Working hard helps to overcomes adversity
Being smart and working hard generates certainty

As long as we continue no matter good or bad
We will make positive steps with each success we add

Nothing is easy and persistence is the key
Nothing is easy nor would we want it to be

John Morgan Mullen

Respect

Respect can't be bought, borrower or learned
It's takes righteous courage and must be earned

Respect is a collection of the hard decisions we've made.
It a reputation of tough choices and the mental prices we've paid.

Our honorable deposits increase our character account.
We continually build and expand our respect amount.

Successful endeavors are the gold standard for respect.
We admire and strive for success in every aspect.

Respect is deeply rooted in both economical and ethical success.
We strive to achieve and attempt to accept no less.

Sometimes respect is gained by how we react to defeat.
Respect is defined by when diversity and character meet.

Winning the battle of your inter-self's heart.
Because Respect for yourself is where it all starts.

Family, friends require us to be compassionate and kind.
With Success, Knowledge, Fairness being the next in line.

More than money, fame or anything you conceive.
Respect is what we all hope to achieve.

John Morgan Mullen

CHAPTER TWO
Dreams, Hope & Love

Hope

Our world is in need of a small dash of hope.
Surrounded by a little faith so we might cope.
Hope that is supported by friends and family every day.
With moments of courage & strength along the way.

Our doctors tell us the cancer drugs will keep us alive.
But not without some mental & emotional hope to survive.
There are medical specialist oversee our serious concerns.
As we fill ourselves with hope and compassion at every turn.

Hope is our best crutch we can find to fight our despair.
To face our fears and minimize our anticipated scare.
With each session, x-ray, scan, we're close to the end of our rope.
Please God provide us with a small magical sliver of HOPE..

John Morgan Mullen

Is it Half Empty or Half Full?

Attitude determines if you're happy or sad.
Inter-peace cannot be achieved when your attitude is bad.

We search for happiness not just material things and money.
When our attitude changes our thunderstorms become sunny.

Don't dwell on the defeats that life brings our way.
But rather the joys and the love we treasure every day.

Things are just things that provide ways to measure.
Cash, houses, cars provide us temporary pleasures.

Attitude plays a big part in improving life's ride.
Is the glass half empty or half full, it's yours to decide.

John Morgan Mullen

The Day the Hope Died

You live life as if it will never end.
As if all pain & sorrow will quickly mend.
We never realize how special our health can be.
With hope that provides a great lifestyle for you and me.

Hope plays a major role in our future dreams.
But hope is only hope and not everything is as it seems.
We attempt to suppress our hopes for fear of disaster.
In our world of chances with fears of the ever after.

But we never know what's life has in store.
How hope and dreams can fly out the door.
As the Doctor utters the words "CANCER"…we cried
And this kick in the ass was the Day Hope Died.

John Morgan Mullen

The Power of WE

As your husband and friend I support you and you support Me.
It goes with life's game that started with You & Me
& progressed to WE.
We became friends, partners & lovers from the start.
Our love has grown and WE are now attached at the heart.

So if you hurt, or if you are sick, or sad, then so am I.
You know how I think, when I'm upset and why I cry.
We have become one as you are now part of Me.
And I am part of you completing the circle back to WE.

WE may not have all the answers to the things WE do.
But the knowledge & strength WE have is the power of two.
Thru the years WE have grown together with love as the key.
It is no longer You or Me, but rather the power of WE.

With Love to You from Me!

John Morgan Mullen

Hope and Love

They say love makes the world go around.
But for many it's the hope that love can be found.

Without love we wallow in selfishness.
Without love all we have is emptiness.

Some are luckier than others in this quest.
So lets' explore the methods that work the best.

Remember "Me first" doesn't work well.
When you fall in love, your status position fell.

To love someone is the 2nd best thing.
To be loved is what make our heart sing.

Hope is eternal and it's worth the wait.
Happiness is dependent upon your fate.

Find that special love and your wish will come true.
Find that special person and your heart will too.

It's the "happy ever after" wish of every man.
As Hope and Love go hand and hand.

John Morgan Mullen

I Promise

I, John, take you Jill, to be my wife.
I hereby renewed today, my promise to love you for life.
I Promise the security of family and friends
A place we are supported and love transcends

I Promise my continued romance with every kiss,
And my appreciation and great joy for my life of bliss.
I Promise truth and happiness, hope and passion.
And pray for strength, patience and compassion.

I Promise faithfulness, honesty and fairness forever
And to be the Man I promised as long as we're together
Our mutual love is far beyond what any heart allows,
As we stand here again reciting our sacred vows.

Please say "I DO"

Love,

John

Power of Thoughts

Thoughts are the product of your mind.
They are powerful, dangerous, and define.

You develop your inner self by what you think.
What you dream, feel, and say are all interlinked.

Stay in control without destroying your creative dreams,
Let your mind go crazy without knowing what it means.

Venture into this unknown world without fear.
As captain of your ship, your job is to steer.

Envision yourself as the star of the team.
Transfer your thoughts into your dream.

Thought becomes actions that make dreams come true—
Inspirational to watch and magical, too.

John Morgan Mullen

Dream World

The quiet dream voice inside your head is a valuable jewel.
It's creative, it's limitless and it's a powerful tool.

Your dream world has very few restrictions.
It's void of barriers, of rules and predictions.

You dream in color and avoid black and white.
The blank canvas is yours, and you paint what you like.

Nothing is impossible if you can dream it to be.
You can make it happen, and believing is the key.

You search your soul, tap your passion, and take it far.
Take control of your life and raise the bar.

Your dreams transform and crystallize your direction.
As benefactor of your dreams, you search for perfection.

Set aside the time to evaluate where you are.
Determine your path and how to become a star.

Dream no small dreams as you reach for the moon.
As you attempt the unthinkable, it will happen soon.

Get out the crystal ball to determine where you want to go,
And paint the picture as if you were Vincent Van Gogh.

Follow your dreams shown in the art,
As it becomes the passion of your heart.

John Morgan Mullen

I Believe I Can Fly

Confidence starts one baby step at a time.
Soon, there won't be a mountain you cannot climb.

You face your challenges every day
With the belief you can fly away.

You develop your beliefs and eliminate your fear,
As your direction and goals become crystal clear.

You will not be afraid of anything new,
As there is nothing you cannot do.

You jump into the darkness and continue to try.
Greatness can be achieved, as I believe I can fly.

John Morgan Mullen

Sex

As a teenager, sex was never far from our mind
We mumbled and fumbled as if we were blind.

We worked hard to find sex, wherever we could
It was perfect, it was beautiful, and it was really good

Then comes the twenties & thirties and thing get even better
Our sexual comfort level and horizons increased since I first met her

Kids are not the death of sex…we learn to compromise
We find the time…we find the place…we learn to improvise

As we mature in our Forties & Fifties we think about sex less
Our lives are filled with schedules, money, work and stress

"Mister Happy" need help as he gets a little older
Supplements & blue pills as we get a little bolder

Our sixties and seventies see our fantasies' diminish
The sex drive is failing before we are even finished

But as we get older we rally ever now and again
It sad, but at times, we are finished before we begin

My mind is willing but the body is not
Memories of better times is the best that I've got

Please understand that sex and love are not the same thing
Sex makes us content but love makes us sing

John Morgan Mullen

I Remember...

I remember "the 1st time ever I saw your face."
That first kiss and the tingle with each embrace.
I remember 1965 was the All-Time Best Fall.
A miracle from heaven brought me to Wonders Hall.

I remember the days of fun, the nights of passion when dreams came true,
Followed by the love and commitment that go hand
& hand with the "I Do".
I remember that Day on June Seventeenth Nineteen Sixty-Seven,
The day I thought I died and went to Heaven.

I remember the mountains of Utah, skyline of Chicago,
the Michigan Lakes,
The Indiana parties, the Children's Museum and even the heart aches.
I remember when standing, I used to be able to see my shoes.
And when "Mister Saturday Night" & "Mister Happy" weren't Old News.

I remember that some of our memories were happy and some sad.
But they were all part of this great journey we've had.
I remember how we lived like there's no tomorrow.
Did the things we loved without regret or sorrow.

I remember how you make my heart sing,
Because you <u>are</u> "the wind beneath my wings."
I remember the kids & grandkids when life moved so fast.
And promise you that we have "saved the best for last".

I remember how 50 Years has gone by way too fast.
Memories of Time, Love & Family...cause WE ARE OUR PAST.
I remember each step of this incredible ride.
And the pleasure of having you by my side.

John Morgan Mullen

What is Love?

Love starts with the sparks that fly with that first kiss,
The passion of that first touch, the anticipation of sexual bliss.
The excitement grows and I can't wait for what comes next!
Two bodies pressing against one another in wild sex!

As my mind races with this crazy sexual anticipation.
Great adoration is exceeded with exploding wet imagination,
Bingo…Hallelujah. Oh please God just don't ever let it end!
In the attempt to repeat the feeling again and again.

In the car, on the floor, find a bed the location doesn't matter.
Until we start to hear those sweet sound of the pitter patter.
As the plot thickens, with commitment as we try and get it right.
Work hard, play hard especially on Saturday night.

The first Chapter of this Love Story deal with Passion
Followed closely with commitments, love and compassion.
Love changes as life lopes along with changes every day.
Sometimes family, job and pressures get in our way

The attachment grow stronger with the passing years
The bond is strengthen through laughter and tears
While the passion guy might be considered over the hill
He shows up sometimes with the help of the little blue pill

Perfect is nowhere to be found, that certainly is clear
The secret of long lasting relationship is simply, "Yes Dear"
With all my faults and imperfections I ask just one more time.
Please consider saying "yes" and please be my Valentine,

John Morgan Mullen

You Had Me at "Hello"

Our years at Michigan State were the best year of my life
The God's of love blessed me when you agreed to be my wife
It was love at first sight and I feared you would say "No"
But the "Love Angels" were kind and "You had me at Hello"

Over 50 years ago these two young and innocent kids blindly fell in love
Life has its own agenda as we learn how to stand tall, fight and shove
As the two of us together fought life's battles as partners & soul mates
We forged ahead in a leap of faith, developing a world that was first rate

It's amazing how the fate of Wonders Hall changed our lives forever
The chance we'd be in the same location at the same time is almost never
Right place and time as I found the pot of love at the end of the rainbow
You changed my world that day as "You had me at Hello"

John Morgan Mullen

One Step at a Time

Hopes and Dream are achieved one step at a time
To give up hopes and dreams would be a crime

We never know what those baby steps might mean
Until we venture one step at a time into our dreams

Sometimes the steps are not always in the right direction
Forward, backwards, left or right as we make corrections

Persistence is essential as success is not a straight line
If we just keep moving forward, we will be just fine.

Disappointments, and there may be many
We address our setbacks until there aren't any

Success is certain when we continue to try
One step at a time is the reason why

John Morgan Mullen

Courage of Change

Venture into the unknown world of change.
Give your life the courage to rearrange.

You either get better or worse, but never stay the same.
So dedicate your efforts to improve your game.

You have three strikes, so use them all.
Don't give up and keep your eye on the ball.

You learn from your mistakes, so don't be afraid to try.
When you step out into the unknown, you learn to fly.

John Morgan Mullen

Change or Die

Change is scary viewed with doubt, anxiety and fear.
But sometimes greeted with happiness, joy and cheer.
We need to prepare for change or we will be passed by.
In order to progress we either change or we die.

Sometimes change is good and sometimes it is bad.
We learn to adapt to both being happy and sad.
Strong values of the heart are the basis of our beliefs.
As cautiously we protect when turning over a new leaf.

Changes comes whether we want them or not.
It's stubborn, it's has a mind of its own and wins a lot.
You choose to fight it or embrace it with hope.
Either way, with change we must learn to cope.

Our world is rapidly changing and do I have a choice?
Maybe I like it the way it is, can I have a voice?
Can I resist change…. I ask myself why.
I can, but it is a matter of Change or Die.

John Morgan Mullen

Grandson & Friend

Dear Brennan

It's not often we get to say my "Grandson & Friend".
As measured by time, laughter & smiles before we say Amen.
Your tragic death will always be with me as it haunts me every day.
I bury myself in grief as I search to find the light to lead my way.

We are friends and that doesn't stop even when you die.
But you left me with this hole in my heart desperately wondering why.
I know you're there, in more than just the spirt of my mind,
As I see you on the pontoon, jet skis and hear your laughter all the time.

I want to invite you to all games between Indiana and Michigan State.
This rivalry generate comradery and shall forever feed our debate.
I think we should have an ongoing bet that lasts forever more.
But you are not allowed to call upon God to fix the score.

Brennan, I will be here for you and you also need to be there for me.
We are friends, so please help me to see, what sometimes, I cannot see.
Our minds and our spirts transform into an alternate heavenly fate.
So please kindly extend your hands in friendship from your heavenly state.

My memories are wonderful but come with a few tears,
Of many great times that will fuel my memories for years.
Please remember our adventures as your New World begins.
You started as my Grandson and progressed to my Friend.

Love,

John Morgan Mullen
(Grandpa)

"It's a Girl"

The most precious gifts are not Money, Gold, Diamonds or Pearls.
But rather the joys, the smiles and kisses from your little Girl.

While you love them all, whether a girl or a boy,
Your little Girl become your bundle of joy.

As you rock her to sleep and look into her eyes… and she blinks,
As if she is saying "I love you Mommy" and your heart just sinks.

She will challenge and test you every day.
It's hard but you wouldn't want it any other way.

She shows you unconditional love in her eyes
As you hold her close and cherish your beautiful little prize

Your little angel will sometimes tear you apart
She will cost you a ton and will steal your heart

So hang on, your world is about to change
Your LOVE category needs to be increased and rearranged

Your little Girl is about to join the your ranks
And God deserves your eternal thanks.

Congratulations

John & Jill

The Mansards Friends

Something special started back in nineteen sixty nine.
At the Mansards in Northwest Indiana just east of Cline.

A group of kids that started partying in the courtyard,
We played, we danced, laughed & drank right in our backyard.

The refrigerator box maze at Haloween party was crazy
And the hospital wheel chair races is still a little hazy.

We move uptown with the Steen's joining our crowd.
Fun was had by all, but maybe just a bit too loud.

Responsibilities grew with kids, jobs and houses too.
We dispersed to other locations and we miss our old crew.

It's now 50 years and we still party, drink, laugh and play
Pretending that the day before yesterday is really today.

These Mansard friendships are special and we had a blast.
Old friends are priceless as we remember our party past.

John Morgan Mullen

The Men of Sparta

The history of football was changed forever.
The assemblage of champions was Duffy's endeavor.
From how football was televised to post season games,
But the integration of players became our "claim to fame."

Brotherhood trumps race and talent was the key.
We started with "I" and progressed to "we."
Two National Championships were the results attained,
But teamwork and comradery were the gifts we gained.

We experienced the thrill of victory with only one "agony of defeat."
In the "Game of the Century" we "kissed our sister"
which was bittersweet.
Our record of 19-1-1 only tells part of the story,
Only our friendships and memories exceeded our glory.

Black or White, super star or white rock, we didn't care.
We fought side by side as a family, which is very rare.
Brotherhood developed as we came together as peers.
Congratulations to the *Men of Sparta* for those incredible years.

John Morgan Mullen "15"

Kids & Kids Kids

We sometimes look back and say "what is our
Purpose in life" and why are we here?
We search for answers, we look for reason,
As we try to understand with mounting fear.

As we progress from kids, trying to find direction,
Hoping and struggling our decisions are right.
We get married and along comes the kids that
Bring joy and purpose as we start to see the light.

We shepherd our Kids from babies to teens, from
Young adults and beyond, searching for what it all means.
Right from wrong, honesty, love, and respect, as family
take center stage as our purpose becomes our dreams.

Next come the Kids Kids and this gives us great
Happiness love and joy that they brings our way.
We play, we laugh, we encourage and love,
We learn and teach each and every day.

The family bond, the love and friendship
Is centered around our family's genes.
"Our Purpose in Life" evolves and unites our family of
Kid & our Kids Kids for this is what it all means.

John Morgan Mullen

Fishing is more than Fish

Fishing is a pleasure that provides me with my mental release.
It's just me and the lake, the fish and the incredible quite & peace.

Work provides my comforts, my family the love but my fishing
is my passion
Fishing is more than Fish, it creatively provides me
my needed distractions

This ritual as ingrained into my world by Dad and his friends.
A magical retreat allowing for reflection as my mind & body mends.

I am grateful to Lief for introducing me a to my Heaven on Earth
As he realized my coping issues, as I am a Norwegian by birth.

Fishing has provided me with my release to my world hectic strife
A way to relieve my pain, rededicate my world and reprioritize my life

My place of solitude that provides me with more than just
catch and release
As fishing is my mental therapy of retreat that gives me
comfort and peace.

John Morgan Mullen
(for Erik Jonasen)

Fly Away

An Eagles mission is to train their young to be independent,
strong and obey.
They teach them the things they need to know and then they fly away.

We nurture our young and prepare them for the
adventures and life's tests
Just as the Eagles, we must gently coax, nudge
and push our babies from the nest

Without fear they must spread their wings and learn to fly
And conquer more opportunities than stars in the sky.

This gentle push teaches them to fly and much more,
As our little Eagles must fly away in order to soar.

John Morgan Mullen

A Dreamer's Promise

The New Years is upon us and we reflect on what we've done.
The good, the bad, but mostly the fun.

We look ahead with promise and hope
Sometimes it seems like we are at the end of our rope.

"Never fall in love with a dreamer" they say
But please hang in there and we will have our Day.

We have made and lost a fortunate of two
And our ships coming in cause it's overdue.

I promise you this.... that our dreams will come true.
The beauty of New Years is that I celebrate it with you.

Together we can do anything my dear.
I promise this will be a very good year.

Happy New Year with love,

John

My Dream For Us

My dream for us is a moonlit boat cruise with a bottle of wine.
A lot of love and laughter with all troubles left behind.
My dream for us is to stay healthy, enjoy our family and have fun.
See our grandkids take over the world before riding off into the sun.

My dream for us is to play until we drop over with laughter.
To get rich, spend money and live happily ever after.
My dream for us is to relive our sexual peak.
And don't stop until we reach that pinnacle we seek.

Take that trip to Italy & France before we visit the Pearly Gates.
Go to Norway and Ireland to see our homelands before it's too late.
My Dream for Us is to celebrate our life together and do it NOW.
As tomorrow is uncertain even if we don't know how.

Hopefully we will conquer our life's battles together.
With Peace and Love thru all kinds of weather.
As we ride into the sunset having all our dreams come true.
We create OUR dreams for US…together for Me and YOU.

With Love,

Me & You

CHAPTER THREE
Politics

Decisions

The decision we make will affect our world for years
It's confusing and complicated which increases our fears

I do my research, evaluate and listen to my voice
I debate the issues inside my head and make my choice

Now you may, or may not agree, but that's what makes us great
I make my decisions based on positions and issues, not who I hate

Our election have been exceptionally cruel
It's ugly, it's dirty and they think I'm a fool

Our problems are many and they are complicated no doubt
We select our best leaders and hopefully they can figure it out

The election is before us and the question is who.
Not sure if it Black, White, Right, Left, Red or Blue?

John Morgan Mullen

I Believe

I believe both Republicans and Democrats want our vote
We select our leaders every four years as the Constitution wrote

I believe our lives are filled with choices we need to make
I'm sorry but I'm not sure which side of the Isle to take

I believe providing food and medicine for those in need
For helping the homeless, the needy or the poor we feed

I believe our tax code is not fair
It's full of loopholes from years of manipulation and wear

I believe in collecting Social Security and Medicare
But our government treats it like its welfare

I believe the election season is excessively long
Presidential campaigns begin before the last one is gone

I believe that to receive welfare a drug test we must take
Maybe an incentive to find work so we have something at stake

I believe we live in a country that we can speak our mind
We can agree and disagree in hopes of a middle ground we might find

I believe that term limits are a must
More time leading from someone we can trust

I believe I have voted both ways, and I am not Red or Blue
I believe my available choices are far too few

John Morgan Mullen

Political Choices

Two Thousand Twenty Presidential Election is at all-time political low
Campaigns have been embarrassingly & brutal cruel
from both Donald and Joe
What we need is leadership on both sides of the isle.
Compromise is the name of our ideal government style.

Economic disaster, worldwide pandemic with 1000's dying everyday
Our country needs direction, compassion and trust
from our leaders today
I've never seen a time with such political divisive attacks
By our Leaders without regards to truth or facts

Tell us what you stand for and not who you hate.
Your platform and vision, not that your opponent is second rate.
Maybe I'm naïve to wish for honesty, compassion and trust,
Character, respect, patience, that's decisive and just.

Maybe we eliminate the loop holes in our tax codes,
We could balance the budget, feed the poor, and fix the roads.
Both Parties point fingers and say it's not their fault
It's time to stand up together and admit this must halt

Can our political leaders bring us together as one voice?
Can they set their egos aside and provide us a fair choice?
Or does the PAC money dictate what they can and can't do.
Because our world is not made up of simply Red or Blue.

My positions are sometimes "Right" and sometimes
"Left, as well as in between.
I have voted both sides and am moderately red, blue and even green
Republican or Democrat, man or women, black or white, we don't care
We desperately need a leader that's strong, objective,
compassionate and fair.

John Morgan Mullen

I Have a Dream

I have a Dream that we have compassionate leaders that are fair.
That inspire our people and lead with truth, honesty and care.

Politics is meant to be a compromising debate of issues
that are worthwhile.
A lively political discussion that creates opinions from
both side of the isle.

But our current political environment is dividing our country with hate.
My dream is that we compromise our differences before it's too late.

I have a Dream of opportunities for all not just gender, nor age
or the color of their skin.
And not where you live, or who you know, but rather your
determination and ability within.

I have a Dream that includes our education being based not
on privilege, but on talent.
That our leaders' vision for greatness inspires our people to be strong
and gallant.

We must be bold and insist that these principals can and will be done.
The Dream MUST be more than a dream, so we may proclaim
that the "People Won".

Our world has evolved into a divisive battle between the "haves" and the "have nots".

The "haves" need to be patience, compassionate and caring and provide the "have-nots" a shot.

I have a Dream that our differences will diminish or cease.
And it's my Dream that we can all live together in peace.

John Morgan Mullen

Political Leader

Does the PAC money dictate what they can and can't do?
Because our world is not made up of simply Red or Blue.

Just because the money says it's right, or it's wrong,
Doesn't mean we all must all sing the same song.

Many of us are neither "Right" nor "Left, as we are in between.
We are moderately red, blue and even green.

We think we need a party that represent our moderate positions.
So we might find a common ground, or is democracy in remission?

While a 3rd party never seems to work well.
We believe that a middle road just might sell.

A platform of decency, fairness and justice for all,
While incentives for business is always a good call.

What we need is leadership on both sides of the isle.
Compromise is the name of our ideal government style.

Maybe I'm naïve to wish for honesty, compassion and trust,
Character, respect, patience, that's decisive and just.

A man or women, black or white, we don't care
A leader that's strong, objective and fair.

We enter the political midterm season with trepidation and hope.
Please God provide us with a leader for our vote.

John Morgan Mullen

Government Stinks

Our lives are filled with choices we need to make
Republican or Democrat which side of the Isle do I take

They all have their agenda... to the hell with the rest
They protect their butts to save their nest

The problems are complicated with ramification on either side
Do they make the right choices...their conscience will decide.

I am socially compassionate yet fiscally conservative
Separate end of the spectrum as I look for alternatives

Understanding the problems are next to impossible
Yet Politicians preach and pretend they are unstoppable

While love has no borders and legal aliens we support
Maybe we should provide our own homeless more comfort

Why are the worlds battle ours to fight
They respect us not, even if we are right

Our men are dying for their regional disputes
It upsets me that our respect they continue to dilute

Welfare is essential, but can be additive
It destroys ambition which is restrictive

As our political world starts to sinks
I'm beginning to wonder if our Government stinks.

John Morgan Mullen

Middle East

Iraq, Algeria, Israel, Sudan,
Yemen, Libya, Syria and Iran,
Ukraine, Palestine, Turkey and Pakistan
Nigeria, Chad, Cameroon and Afghanistan.

Not sure who's the good guys and who's the bad
The region is a nuclear missile on the launch pad.
We give the good guys support and we die for their cause
And they hate us, our religion and our laws

Hamas, Boko Haram, Al-Qaeda or ISIS,
Terrorist bombings, beheadings, there's always a crisis
The region is a hot bed for radical insanity
For illogical actions against humanity

Hatred and jealousy of our Western ways,
Their Barbaric actions astonish and amaze.
Boko Haram, ISIS they all believe we live in sin
Hatred for Americans... how can we win?

There are 185 terrorist groups throughout the area
Extremist Religious Idiots causes this hysteria
There must be countries with stability, if even only a few
But I fear the bad guys are winning and then what do we do

Isolationism sounds good but it doesn't work
Our world needs sanity when working with jerks
It's an incredible problem as we search for the solutions
Hopefully we can find it without more horrible revolutions.

John Morgan Mullen

Patriotic American

As a patriotic American I feel the obligation to vote.
It's my chance to voice my opinion as the Constitution wrote.

Primary campaign season is upon us very soon.
Politicians are constantly campaigning and promising the moon.

Republican or Democrat my choices are few.
The pontificating rhetoric is deafening, is it Red or is it Blue?

I have voted both ways and I fear it doesn't matter.
While our politicians move their lips it's mostly useless chatter.

The shit is bantered from one side of the isle to the other.
That's why politics stink, as they get shit on each other.

Tell us what you stand for and not who you hate.
Your platform and vision and not that your opponent is second rate.

Republican, Democrat, Independent, I hope they succeed.
A man, women, black or white, I just want someone to lead.

So make our County proud, play nice and keep it clean,
And don't neglect your job between now and November, 2016.

John Morgan Mullen

Dear Politician, I'm Sorry

Our lives are filled with choices we need to make
I'm sorry but I'm not sure which side of the Isle to take
Republicans and Democrats, they want our vote
We select our leaders every four years as the Constitution wrote

I've voted both ways, and I am not Red or Blue
I'm sorry but my available choices are far too few
I'm sorry but Understanding the problems are next to impossible
Yet Politicians preach and pretend they are unstoppable

The problems are complicated with ramification on either side
Do they make the right choices...their conscience must decide.
I am a middle of the road guy that can't afford a Ferrari
Fiscal conservative yet social compassionate and I'm Sorry, I'm not Sorry

I'm sorry I'm not sorry for providing food and medicine for those in need
For helping the homeless, the needy or the poor we feed
I'm sorry I'm not sorry for believing our tax code is not fair
It's full of loopholes from years of manipulation and wear

I'm sorry I'm not sorry for collecting Social Security and Medicare
But it's my money, I lent the government and I'm treated like its welfare
I'm sorry but I don't like the category of middle class,
The politician better listen or we might just give them a pass

I'm sorry I don't feel sorry for the wealthy with their
excesses they've spent
I do appreciate the jobs and congratulate them for being
in the One percent
I'm sorry I'm not sorry for thinking the election season
is excessively long
Presidential campaigns begin before the last one is gone

I'm sorry that the world's battles seem to be ours to fight
They respect us not, even if we are right
I'm sorry that our men are dying in their regional disputes
It upsets me that our respect they continue to dilute

I'm sorry but I believe that to receive welfare a drug test we must take
Maybe an incentive to find work so we have something at stake
I'm not sorry for my hatred of radical terrorist in the name of Jihad
I have a problem with anyone that kills in the name of their God

I'm not sorry that we live in a country that we can speak our mind
That we can agree and disagree in hopes of a middle ground
we might find
I'm sorry but I think that term limits are a must
And we require more great leaders that we can trust.

I'm sorry but please tell us what you stand for not who you hate
Tell us your platform and not that your opponent is second rate.
Good Luck in November as we wish you the best
And I am sorry that you must clean up this terrible mess.'

John Morgan Mullen

War

War is ridiculous
War brings pain
War is for idiots
War is insane

What does it prove
I ask myself why?
Little is accomplished
And many will die

Ukraine has been devastated
Russia has torn it apart
They fight for their homeland
As it's stripped from their hearts.

They defend their State
Throughout the fight
Are proud and dedicated
And stand up for what's right

They are strong and gallant
Dedicated and full of pride
As they defeat their Goliath
On the other side.

John Morgan Mullen

Chapter Four
Special Occasions

Happy "I DO"

I loved you even before the "I do".
And value every year that I have spent with you.
If we were to get married again now...what would I say?
"I promise I'll do better this time" as I wash all the bad times away.

Our love was destined for greatness with happiness together.
You have made me who I am & I will love you forever.
Our Love & strength of our marriage, have very few peers.
We experienced a growing and powerful bond thru 51 years.

We chose adventure as appose to stability.
Recklessness as appose to tranquility.
Our life has been complicated as appose to simple.
Our home has been modest as appose to a Temple.

No matter where we lived, No matter rich or poor,
No matter what we did, I couldn't have asked for more.
Together, we never feared, but welcomed change.
Our life together, I would never exchange.

The joy provided by our kids and grandkids can never be measured.
They are our life blood and they will forever be treasured.
I'm excited as we plan for the years ahead.
It's less amount money but comfort instead.

With hat in hand, as we celebrate our passions together.
I freely give and ask for your LOVE...again...Forever!

Happy Anniversary
Snuggie Bear

Anniversary Number Forty-nine

We're experts as we've done this for a while.
It's been forty-nine years since we walked down the aisle.

We've been good and bad, right and wrong,
We've been weak and sometimes strong.

We've been up and down, happy and sad,
Imperfect but thankful for what we had.

We've got a great life, even though we often disagree,
Black or white, together we have created our destiny.

We're not rich, but then we're not poor.
More time, please, before you kick me out the door.

We have not played it safe, that's for sure,
But our mutual love has always been pure.

My wish is for happiness and good health,
Laughter, friends, family and wealth.

So what can we do that we haven't already done?
My wish is to play more and just have more fun.

Happy 49th Anniversary
Love,

Snuggie Bear

Happy Anniversary (2014)

I can't believe we've been married so long
Your love and patience has been so strong
I have been a challenge and thank you for not giving up
I'm surprised you didn't require some sort of Pre-Nup

Chicago, Indiana, Utah and MSU
We've lived many places and loved them all too
The years have passed in a blink of the eye
My love for you has grown and I'm a lucky guy

The best is still ahead of us so please hang in there
We are perfect for each other and make a great pair
It's been forty-seven years with help from above.
Happy Anniversary….as I offer you all my love.

Morgan

Happy Anniversary— "53"

I am sure of very few things throughout my life.
But it was certainly the best decision, to ask you to be my wife.
You had an array of choices & I was a 3-point underdog at best.
You have no idea how happy you made me when you said…"YES".

We were stupid & and didn't know what our life would bring.
We were young and innocent but knew we had the real thing.
MSU was the place where the magic began.
The parties, the sex and the fear of Viet Nam.

Our lives brought work, new friends, laughter and party time.
Together we took on the world and didn't have a dime.
We assembled our team of Todd, Stephanie, you and me.
Our first few adventures we were young and free.

Westmont, Indiana, Michigan, Utah, Chicago and Canadian lakes
Love commitments, hard work, passion, friends & whatever it takes
The result of our passion were Stephanie and Todd.
With our Grandkids being our presents from God.

We worked hard as we learned that nothing is free.
Our lessons were many but mutual Love was the key.
We experienced the best and the worst of what we choose.
Sometimes we win life's game and sometimes we lose.

Love is the thing and you can't buy with diamonds or gold.
It's the most precious of gifts that can't be bought or sold.
For-Fifty-Two Years we have taken it, and given it for free.
So please consider renewal of my Love in Fifty-Three.

John Morgan Mullen

Anniversary Love

You found the secret of "How to keep the love Alive."
How to have fun, work hard, play, and survive.

You are our heroes and role models and you've showed us the way.
We thank you and wish you the best on this special day.

Life is not easy and struggles you share,
Overcome by your love which is very rare.

Anniversary Love with very few peers.
Congratulations on a fantastic fifty-two years.

Love,

John & Jill

Birthday Formula

Age is a scientific formula that is determined by time.
Years can be added or subtracted from life's prime.

Credit is given with each bit of laughter.
Penalties are levied with every disaster.

Keep track of the kind deeds as they are worth a lot.
You can use them to erase time for diseases you got.

Sex is the greatest drug discovery in our life.
When taken often it adds years for both husband and wife.

Age by the number of years is important to no one.
We prefer to count the friends, family, kids and the fun.

So the higher the number the more we play.
We wish you a happy & healthy Birthday.

Love you,

John & Jill

New Year's Dreams

I had a dream last night that it was 2017.
We were on the beach in Mexico…a fabulous scene.
As we were lounging around watching the sunset,
We officially have become part of the jet set.

The dream continued thru an incredible year.
2017 promises greatness…"bartender bring me another beer."
Sex, Money, cars, houses and fame,
"Oh God please don't wake me, it would be a shame."

The setting in Chapter 2 was Vatican City which was hard to beat.
"Oh shit! We're in Rome Honey…this dream is sweet."
We're sitting in a small outdoor café sipping wine.
The historic architecture, restaurants everything is divine.

The Dream of 2017 is filled with success and money.
Good health, travel, family and everything is sunny.
We've had our share of the bad and now is the time for the good.
It's been hard, but our problems are behind us, as well they should.

As I awake from this yearlong celebration dream,
Together, you and I make the "perfect team."
So I raise my Pina Colada glass to you,
As we make all our New Year dreams come true.

Happy New Year with Love,

Snuggie Bear

Special Christmas Gift

-He did it again-

Jill, so what did John get you for a Christmas Gift?
He's so generous and always gives our spirt a lift.

Did he get you something expensive and fun,
Something that had to cost him a ton.

Or maybe a trip to the Caribbean that would be nice.
Or some diamonds or pearls or something at a high price.

Well, he really out did himself this year.
He's so romantic and is such a dear.

No, this year he really reached for the highest star.
He took me to Mt Pleasant to wash my car.

Merry Christmas with love,

Mr. Pondscum

Another Birthday...Another Year

It's old hat….another Birthday…another year
Welcome to "the game of the seventies" my dear

Old age creeps in and I think you've officially there
But Cuddled alongside your very own Snuggy Bear

But seventy doesn't have to be full of gloom & doom
You now have time to play and let the fun resume

A nap in the hammock, or an afternoon on the boat
A fun day trip or maybe just a pontoon float

Travel is always a great goal to pursue
Passports are updated, and it's long overdue

Years are just chapters in your life's story
A book of triumphs, accomplishments and glory

You deserve much more than I can afford to pay
My gift is my love and my wish for a Happy Birthday

Love,

Snuggy Bear

Dear Jill

It's Hard to Say Goodbye

Our time has been filled with love and now ends in a blink of the eye.
My love for you can't just be turn off and…"it's hard to say goodbye".

You "had me at hello" and "Til Death Due Us Part" does not apply
We will live side by side forever, as our love will never die.

I loved you since the Summer of Nineteen Six-five
And throughout our life and beyond death as our love will survive

We chased that shining star, searching for that brass ring.
We took chances and were not afraid to spread our wings.

Together we faced Life's challenges at every turn,
As our love developed with lessons that were hard earned

Not sure if I can make it without you by my side.
As you're love has been there for me every step of this great ride.

You are my love and my life and with a tear in my eye.
I'll love you forever and "It's Hard to say Good Bye".

With Love,

Your very own Snuggie Bear

Christmas is But Once a Year

Christmas time comes but once a year.
It brings with it merry times and great cheer.

A time for laughter and memories galore,
When we remember why we love and much more.

It's not the presents but what they represent,
It's not the size or what we've spent.

It's made up of the fun and stories of Christmas past.
Of stories and presents that have been a blast.

Like the unexpected Angola Christmas delight,
Or the Utah Christmas scenery that was out of sight.

Michigan full house with family and all it's fun,
Like pulling Santa out of the snowbank…I'm sorry Hon.

It's not the money or the successes we remember,
But rather the feeling of joy and blessings in late December.

Christmas is a time for reflections of the love and joys,
Of our Family and friends and not the toys.

It's our health, it's our joys, it's our love and our hopes,
it's our family, it's our dreams and how we cope.

I've loved you throughout the years with all my might,
So, Merry Christmas to all and to all a Goodnight.

Morgan

Happy Birthday Wish

We often wonder what happen to the years
Kids, family, friends, houses, cars and careers

The day before yesterday we were carefree and young
Remember our sexual revolution when the love bug stung

But you are only sixty seven and I'm only sixty nine,
So let's have fun while the moon and the stars are in align

Lets' make the next ten years the best they can be
We can have fun together just you and me

Lets' revive date night and work on Our Bucket list
Double check our dreams so nothing is missed

So lets' play hard and have fun, honey
My gift to you is a lot of love wrapped in a little money

Love,

Morgie

Dear Mom

Mother's Day is a celebration between Mother and Child.
Their Love is the strongest Bond that can ever be complied.
This LOVE is an emotion that continues beyond our last breath.
Our mutual love grows <u>forever,</u> even beyond life and death.

Nothing is more powerful as the special feeling is maternal.
Our hearts are forever joined in bloodlines that are eternal.
We are joined by more than blood but by a forever lifeline.
With memories that bind the hearts of yours and mine.

You played a Hugh role in my entire life's fate.
And it won't be long that we reminisce at the Gate.
I think of you often and wish there was a way
That I could hug you one more time on this Mother's Day.

With Love,

John

MSU 50 Years

We just celebrated our 50 year Anniversary of our MSU team.
Two national championships, oh how we did beam.

While many couldn't make it, as their game clock ran out.
But they were there in spirt and looking down on us no doubt.

You paraded us around with accolades galore.
They showered us with gifts, receptions, speeches and more.

We rekindled the friendships that anchored those days.
We were fierce and competitive in so many ways.

Thanks to President Simon, Mark Hollis, Coach Dantonio and his staff,
To Con, Micki and Ernie for organizing this celebration on our behalf.

The Presidents reception, tailgate and game seats were great.
You made us heroes for a day and that we appreciate.

The comradery & friendship continue thru the years.
It was a great gathering of teammates, friends and peers.

Fifty years dims the line between stars and rocks.
We fondly remember the days when we were all just jocks.

So thanks to all those involved in throwing this party.
Your efforts are appreciated from our heart of Sparty.

MSU 1965 & 1966 Football Team

John Morgan Mullen "15"

Lowell's Dash

The dates listed on your tombstone are separated by a tiny "Dash"
This Dash contains your entire world & your life's memories to rehash

The money you make will be forgotten after it's spent
But Friends and Family will remember what your life really meant

Your "Dash" is filled with the happy, the sad, the laughter and tears
It's full of love for family and friends throughout the years

Your "Dash" was huge and was embellished in nineteen sixty-nine
By a group of Mansard residence that perfected the party time

We will hear your friends and loved one reminisce
about the good old days
When life was good and we were all healthy as we entered our final phase

As the infectious laughter continues after fifty years
As our final hooray and continued party spirts nears

Duane, David and Judy Panazzo can introduce you to God
So, ask "HER" if you can reserve the bar for the Mansard party squad

The loving friendships that have developed over the years
Are the result of the love for fun that has been establish among our peers

Lowell, you were our Captain, our leader our doctor and our friend
We will all be there shortly, but just don't quite know when

With Great Love and Respect,
Your Loving Friends

Merry Christmas Gifts

Ok, so what do I get Jill for Christmas this year?
Something special that maybe will bring a tear.
But tears are not good, I need something happy and fun.
Maybe money, jewelry, but that will likely cost a ton.

Ok, so use Florida trip, that would be smart.
"You're an Asshole and just confirmed you ARE a dumb fart."
I need a once in a lifetime present that says "wow".
But it sounds expensive and I can't afford it right now.

Last year's present was a necklace made from magic rocks.
Never worn, total disaster and I'm a dumb jock.
Over the years I have found expensive jewelry to do the trick.
Thank God for Roger's Jewelers cause they are my best pick.

Christmas allows us to share our love with family and friends.
To celebrate, to laugh, to love and to make amends.
To remember the great times from Christmas past.
The great people and friendship that will forever last.

We've celebrated Christmas thru the years in some magical places.
Christmas in college, Michigan Ave parade, and the Utah Ski races.
I wish you a Merry Christmas and a Happy New Year too,
As Christmas always reminds me of my love for you.

Merry Christmas with Love,
Snuggie Bear

Happy Birthday & Happy Mother's Day

Do I dare try to combine her Birthday and Mother's day?
You'd be an idiot to even try it and my advice is "NO WAY!"
OK, but what can I get her this year?
Something special to overcome the car wash fear.

Maybe flowers and a poem that would be nice.
You are a dumb ass but I do like the price.
How about a new house, diamonds or cars.
She deserves the best so shoot for the stars!

OK… a trip next winter, cause that would be fun.
Expensive and warm so we can play in the sun.
Get real asshole…that's a year away.
She deserves more…and it's gotta be today!

The "she's not My Mother" thing does not work.
It's a guaranteed title of "The World's Biggest Jerk".
Ok "Mr Got Rocks" so what do you have in mind?
Something nice, beautiful and maybe outside the line.

I can't spend a fortunate on the gold, pearls or diamond ring.
But maybe I can appeal to the "cute" love thing.
Special days should be celebrated with LOVE as the key.
They should be fun, happy & all about YOU & WE.

It's got to be special to match my beautiful wife.
Against advice, I combined two important days in your life.
My gift this year is a bundle of Love, for you Honey.
With hugs & kisses & wrapped in money.

Happy Birthday & Happy Mother's Day

Love, Snuggy Bear

Happy Valentine's Day
True Love

True Love is generally initiated by that sensually passionate bliss.
That was created by that powerful and magical moment of that first Kiss

Loves trial and error are endless, as we experienced the ups and downs.
But it's fantastic and beautiful and "Magical" when True Love is found.

And certainly, the memories of those occasions are our glue that binds.
With Love that develops thru the years and is strengthened with time.

True Love is loving a person even at times of hurt and pain.
We regroup, say we're sorrow and together we make it thru the rain.

The trial period for True Love starts prior to "I Do" and never ends.
And extends throughout our lives as we celebrate and make amends

Valentine's Day is a celebration of Love that is True.
So, Please say "Yes" and be my Valentine, because… "I Love You."

With Love,

John

Happy 50ᵗʰ Anniversary

An Anniversary of Fifty Years…so what does it mean?
A successful love affair that few have ever seen.

Dreams that were formulated for a happy life.
Filled with kids & grandkids as husband and wife.

The first chapter of this love story is filled with passion.
Followed closely with commitment, love and compassion.

You've discovered the secret to keeping love alive.
Thru humor, friendship and laughter love will thrive.

The "Perfect Marriage" truly has no peers.
The secret to a good marriage is simply "Yes Dear".

So what can you do that you haven't already done?
Worry less, play more and just have more fun.

May you enjoy those memories of that special Day.
And the joys your life together has brought your way.

Happy Anniversary,
Love,

John & Jill

Christmas Love

Christmas comes but once a year,
It's a time of love and a little cheer.

What makes it special is the thought,
And not the present that we've bought.

Throughout the seasons you're a part of me,
But especially around the Christmas tree.

Christmas pasts have come and gone,
I thank you for taking me along.

From friends we've made to and the laughter we've shared,
The places we've live and the risks we've dared,

Our Christmas love continues to grow,
As you ARE my Christmas love…you know!

All my Love,

John

(Congratulations Joyce)
It's MY Time

My whole life has been marching to the beat of the
drums of everybody but ME.
And now is my chance to spread my wings and be whatever I want to be!

It gives me an opportunity to research my soul and redirect my direction.
A chance that I get but once in a lifetime in attempt to find my perfection.

I review those passions to find & complete the last chapter of my soul.
It's relaxing, it's exciting and it's scary, but total
happiness is my main goal.

I leave behind a world that was pressure packed, hectic
and took its toll on my life.
As I look forward to the peace, and quiet
and elimination of all the strife.

It's now my time to spend fun time with Family and friends.
Spend money on me and all my beautiful sins.

Certainly take trips that are happy and fun,
Laugh, play in the hammock in the sun.

Retirement is great and I'm still in my Prime
As I have paid the price and now IT'S MY TIME!

Congratulation Joyce, Happy Retirement!

John Morgan Mullen

A Dreamer's Promise

The New Years is upon us and we reflect on what we've done.
The good, the bad, but mostly the fun.

We look ahead with promise and hope
Sometimes it seems like we are at the end of our rope.

"Never fall in love with a dreamer" they say
But please hang in there and we will have our Day.

We have made and lost a fortunate or two
And our ships coming in cause it's overdue.

I promise you this, that our dreams will come true.
The beauty of New Years is that I celebrate it with you.

Together we can do anything my dear.
I promise this will be a very good year.

Happy New Year with love,

John

Please say "YES"

Please say "yes" to my simple request.
Please say "yes" and eliminate my stress.
You have the choice…it's entirely up to you.
Please say "yes" so I can make all our dreams come true.

So please say "yes" just one more time.
Please…please won't you be mine.
I have loved you forever, thru both good and bad.
And if you said "No" I would be really sad.

Please say "yes" as you are one of a kind.
So, please say "Yes" and I promise I won't screw up this time.
I love you today, tomorrow and forever.
So please say "Yes" or my heart will sever.

Whatever it takes I'm willing to do.
You are my lover and best friend too.
So I ask you again, please be mine.
So please say "Yes" and be my Valentine.

Love,

John

Gift of Love

My gift to you is my Christmas Love right from the heart.
It's a thing of beauty, a work of art.
Wrapping this present has been a chore.
It won't fit in the package available at the store.

So I looked for a box that would expand over time.
And I will wrap it in kindness that didn't cost me a dime.
It's not diamonds or pearls or expensive gifts galore.
So I packaged it with love for the girl I adore.

Now maybe you will like it, but maybe not.
But if you accept it would mean a lot.
It's endless…it's priceless, so they say.
My gift to you is my Love on this Christmas Day.

Love,

John

Love Grows with Time

We've spent our lives together with love in our heart.
That has grown with the years, right from the start.
June 17, 1967 was a long, long time ago.
As my wish for love was beyond the rainbow.

We have made it thru the good and the bad
For fifth-four years, with many good years to add.
But you are my heart and you are my soul.
As we still have some things to accomplish to achieve our goal.

"Me & you Kid", let's have some fun with the time left on our clock.
You will always been my playmate, as you are my "Rock".
I thought it was impossible to love you anymore.
But we have more love to give, cause it's only fifty-four.

Happy Anniversary
Love,

Morgan

The Power of ME

My Mom & Dad were my coaches throughout my younger years.
THEY taught ME that life brings an assortment of both
happiness and tears.

And that good is good, but great is what we should attempt to BE.
And THEY taught ME that the difference in good
and great start with ME.

THEY instilled in ME that only ME, can make MY fears go away.
And that only ME can make the difference of what I want to BE.

THEY taught ME that, WE ARE what WE allow ourselves to BE.
And that it's MY life, it's MY choice and it all begins with ME.

I will cherish throughout my life these words of wisdom to ME.
That MY happiness and success all start with ME.

Thanks Mom & Dad,
With Love,

ME

Chapter Five
Final Chapter

The Winter of Our Life

Our world is full of Seasons that define the stages of our life.
This journey has been full of great joy for myself and my wife.
We are in the Winter of our Life and have enjoyed each seasons themes.
Our experiences have provided us with the opportunity
to follow our dream.

Spring, Summer and Fall provided us the memories of yesterday,
Allowing us to create the life that has enabled us to come all this way.
On one hand we feel our seasons will never end as time
moves ever so slow.
And then at the same time we wonder where did all the time go?

Winter is the final season of our life's bucket list.
We must identify the dream, pursue them and persist.
Our time is limited so write down your dreams and check 'em twice.
As we have but one shot to achieve our final season of Paradise.

The end is evitable but we just don't know when.
Life's gifts are full of accomplishments and dreams
that end with Amen.
If you do not have a "Bucket List" please develop one today.
As those unfulfilled dreams will die with us along the way.

The Winter of our Life is filled with tasks left undone.
That requires more time as the countdown has already begun.
It almost guarantee we won't be able to do them all.
So we must prioritize every steps both big and small.

Some dreams will never be accomplish and that's not our fault.
As some will forever be locked deep into our life' mental vault.
We have spent all our seasons together as husband and wife.
We made our choices and now celebrate the Winter of our Life.

John Morgan Mullen

Our Retirement World

As we age in our retirement world of Today.
We miss, with mixed emotions, our business world of yesterday.
"The thrill of victory" we celebrate the joys of our success.
As we remember the "Agony of Defeat" which we detest.

Our hectic schedules were maddening, challenging and cruel
We learned to prioritize, organize and loved the delegation tool.
Leaving behind the hectic schedules, pressures and craziness.
Retirement brings, peace & quiet and well-earned laziness.

No meetings, no appointment and no deadline to make.
No phone call, no payroll, no pressure or money at stake.
Play like there's no tomorrow as there might not be.
Relax, enjoy, love, and have fun is our happiness key.

Our ex-work world is peaceful but our health world is a mess.
We can now see the end of the line and all we can do is guess.
We don't dare dwell on this scenario as it will eat us alive.
We rather stay healthy and play until we're at ninety-five.

We're entering the final stretch that we've lived to the max.
The hard truth is that it's almost over and time to relax.
Our world was full of laughter and we've enjoyed the ride.
As I look back with fond memories of you by my side.

John Morgan Mullen

Road Map to Tomorrow

Our objective is to evaluate our technology for our future years.
To Increase our preparation and knowledge to eliminate fears.

Technology has exploded with computers, robotics,
and autonomous cars,
With 3-D printing, stem cell research and exploring the stars.

The jobs of yesterday may cease to exist or will seriously decline.
Employment opportunities change, as our road is never a straight line.

So crawl inside your head and examine your goals.
Your choices, education and passions all plays huge roles.

You must find your niche in those disciplines that will be hot.
As your future comes whether you are prepared or not.

Our road map and research provides us the certainty of knowing.
As it's easier to get there if you know where you're going.

John Morgan Mullen

Getting Old

As a young man I journeyed through life as if it never ends.
I was strong, healthy & active and my body quickly mends.
As the days became years I realize I was no longer a boy.
I took for granted my health, happiness, my love and joy.

Thru my younger years and into adulthood, money was king.
It was the thing I thought was important and made me sing.
Looking forward I was convinced the future would never arrive.
But as I look back I just thank God I'm still alive.

I thought I was invincible and the world belongs to me.
But life teaches us that sometimes it's just not meant to be.
The wisdom of age made me realized the error of my ways.
There is no free lunch and eventually we all must pay.

I will forever remember the experiences of my prime.
With my memories continually detailing the lessons of time.
The years allow for the entire story to unfold.
I truly cherish the past but enjoy getting old.

John Morgan Mullen

Retirement for a Guy like Me

I was thinking, what is retirement for a guy like me?
I know it's not counting my money or playing golf like
I thought it would be.
Or traveling the world, living in the ivory tower,
or siting under a palm tree.
So what is retirement...for a guy like me?

Is it sitting back and collecting a check every now and again,
Or maybe getting more active and making new friends.
Maybe playing with the grandkids or lending a hand,
Or professionally working longer because I can.

I like what I do so maybe I should stay.
Maybe work part time every other day
I would like to travel but not a lot,
Or donate my time, because that I've got.

Maybe mentoring...that might be fun.
Watching them progress as I walk off into the sun
Showing the way as I search my soul
By helping others to achieve their goals

Establish a bucket list, that's what I will do.
Things like adventure, travel, family and friends too.
To play with people and have people play with me.
This will be retirement...for a guy like me?

John Morgan Mullen

How Old is Old?

It's amazing how old age changes as we get older.
Our Time clock moves quicker, faster and bolder.

Old Age is always into the future and not where we are today.
Together with friends that age at the same speed the same way.

And that we will forever be younger than our elders by far,
Guaranteeing that old age is always older than we are.

When we are young, we can't wait til life is at its peak
With old age, far-far into never-never-land we hesitate to seek.

But the passage of time has a way of increasing Age's speed.
Faster and faster with the expiration of our lifetime deed.

The rainbow follows the storm and then the sunshine appears,
As Old Age approaches it is just life's memories followed by years.

John Morgan Mullen

Closer to the Unknown

One look into the doctor's eyes and I knew,
That my new world became more imminent and true.

As the words CANCER slipped out of his lips
My heart stopped as my new reality hits

Some of my previous objectives are but outdated things.
As Love surpasses money and health develops wings.

Adjustments may be needed to my priorities of the past.
And honoring life's fond memories which is an emotional task.

I need to rewrite my goals, examine my life, reminisce and pray.
As I get closer to the unknown, I find I have more things to say.

John Morgan Mullen

Beyond Life & Death

Mother's Day is a celebration between Mother and Child.
Their Love is the strongest Bond that can ever be complied.
This LOVE is an emotion that continues beyond our last breath.
Our mutual love grows <u>forever,</u> even beyond life and death.

Nothing is more powerful as the special feeling is maternal.
Our hearts are forever joined in bloodlines that are eternal.
We are joined by more than blood but by a forever lifeline.
With memories that bind the hearts of yours and mine.

You played a Hugh role in my entire life's fate.
And it won't be long that we reminisce at the Gate.
I think of you often and wish there was a way
That I could hug you one more time on this Mother's Day.

Happy Mother's Day with Love,

John

Illusions & Dreams

Is there a time in which we must lose the illusions of our youth?
Do we set aside our dreams in favor of practicality,
certainty and truth?
We must crawl inside our head and get acquainted
with "the talent guy".
We organize and identify these illusions and dreams
and evaluate and try.

We need to understand the way the game is played.
The way we utilize our talents and how they are made.
We evaluate opportunities and decide is it "yes" or is it "no".
The decisions are many and YOU must decide which way to go.

But illusions have the chance to grow and become your magic key,
That opens the gates to a world of possibilities that allow you to see.
You will always have naysayers that will attempt to bring you down.
As they are all nothing but small men with no ambition to be found.

Dreams sometimes become reality and sometimes not.
They have potential to create success, so give 'em it a shot.
We do not realize what conclusion our illusions might bring.
Your world of dreams and illusion could make your life sing.

John Morgan Mullen

Ok....What's Next

Ok, so what's next before I say Goodbye?
Is there anything left to accomplish before I die?

I'm 76 but not ready to stop playing the game.
And without another chapter is would be a shame.

Medical science has enabled us to live longer.
With our life spans that are healthier and stronger.

Maybe continuing playing the game just one more time.
But the risks are high and I might end up without a dime.

So, "No" I think I'll sit back and enjoy the ride.
Play, write, mentor and all things on the low risk side.

Technologies are expanding the possibilities of "what's next".
Better lives thru health, drugs, robotics and even sex.

John Morgan Mullen

After the Game

My younger years were spent playing the game.
My passion for athletics provided with small moments of fame.

We played the game as part of a team.
A group of athletes with a common theme.

The objective was to achieve perfection again and again.
By developing skills and executing our plan to win.

Leadership and character is developed as team sports require.
With a moral compass that directs, humbles and inspires.

We start with "I" and progress to "WE."
As team sports success is NOT achieved by a "ME."

It prepares our lives with lessons that brought us the fame.
As we surround ourselves with life's memories "After the Game".

John Morgan Mullen

Our strength is in our Body & Mind

Just as the body grows stronger with physical workouts and pain,
Our mind is strengthen with mental exercises that utilizes the brain.
We may find that both require dedication and perseverance to grow.
To increase the stamina and absorb the knowledge as we go.

One might think that the physical workout is harder
than the mental exercise.
But ideally our creative juices and physical talents
should all be equalized.
The joint strength make up the total power of our body and soul.
It's what and who we are, it make us strong or weak, empty or whole.

The mind and the body makes up what's inside and out.
It creates the "who we are" and helps to eliminates all doubt,
Adversity and defeat together with happiness
and joy occur as we cross the line.
As we discover our true self when we crawl inside
our body and our mind.

John Morgan Mullen

Family

Family is our beginning, it's our base and it's who we are.
It's a powerful bond that grows stronger whether near or far.
Our family is spreads throughout our world with love and affection.
With joy and pride as we all long for that family connection.

Family is the joyful sounds of the pitter patter over the years.
We add members and expand to our family with great cheers.
Be it Mullen, Burnard, Kulik, Jonasen, Donegan or Clark,
Or maybe even those furry little animals that purr or bark.

Family is Moms, Dads, Brothers & Sisters, Daughters & Sons,
It's our Grandkids, our pets, it's our friends and all our loved ones.
Family is strength, our anchor and is our biggest plus.
We love our family and our family loves us.

John Morgan Mullen

The Love of My Life

You threw caution to the wind when you agreed to be by wife.
Together we created our world as you were the Love of My Life

How do I go on, as I watch my world being torn apart?
Your death leaves only memories of our life's work of art.

I'm not sure I can make it without you by my side.
Without your love and support through 54 year as my bride.

With you by my side, my life had clarity and the ability to cope.
But now, I have lost every sliver of directions and hope.

So how do I proceed as you were my "everything"
right from the start?
I miss you, I'm afraid, scared and alone with this knife in my heart.

We walked throughout our lives with little thought of tomorrow.
Hand n' hand together with love, victory, defeat and sorrow.

All I have now are our great memories as husband and wife.
And the incredible joys together as "The Love of My Life."

With Love,

John

The Push

The baby eagles are pushed from their nest and forced to fly.
Their Mothers providing a survival nudge or they would die.

They learn early that difficult choices must be made
And to soar among the clouds is the price that must be paid.

They discover their wings with freedom being the key.
To fly, explore and venture throughout their world free.

We can learn a great deal from our eagle friend.
We must Push our kids from their nests so their life may begin.

John Morgan Mullen

Those Left Behind

When our bodies no longer exist, what happens to our
thoughts and our minds?
But our memories have great potential to live forever
and they will be left behind.

With joy together with sadness we celebration what would
have been your Birthday #18.
And remember those fun times that were some of the
greatest we've ever seen.

Brennen, your physical self may have died, but our memories live on.
Our love will live on in our hearts & mind forever
of all those that are gone.

We miss you and there isn't a day that goes by that
we don't think of you and cry.
Thinking about your possibilities, together with our memories,
and struggle with why.

But, if death might only be final for our bodies and not our mind,
Then we can still celebrate all those memories we've made
and you left behind.

So we celebrate YOU on YOUR Birthday as if there's no tomorrow.
But we continue to celebrate our LOVE as if there is…
to help ease our sorrow.

Love you…because there IS a TOMORROW!

Love, Grandpa

The Day Grief Dies

Grief is a natural result of a loss of someone that tears us apart.
It's that internally destructive feeling that is like a knife in your heart.
The wounds that are a natural result and will stay with you
for a long time.
While the pain becomes familiar, they say we can learn
to leave the tears behind.

I will forever remember the feeling as I look into your eyes.
With love and happiness before this terrible disease
required our goodbyes.
Or Brennan's departure that cut deep into our soul.
As we desperately search for anything that can ever refill that hole.

When the most important things in our lives are taken away.
We need to pick ourselves up, get back in the game and find our way.
I am told that the tears will fade, as laughter and smiles
will eventually rise.
As WE remember the laughs and good times as they become
"The Day Grief Dies"

With love,

John

"Jill"...Jill...are you there?"

Each morning when I awake, I ask, "Jill...Jill are you there?"
I feel like you are with me up there somewhere.
My world is hard; it's insane and lonely every day.
I miss you as my wife & friend in every way.

You may not talk, or answer my questions, but I know you're there.
I see your face; I hear your voice, I feel your presence everywhere.
I dream that you are by my side throughout the day.
I'm attempting to go about my life without losing my way.

If your spirit has the opportunity to come back for visits let me know.
I would love to feel you by my side, even if it's just "hello".
We know that after death our physical bodies are no longer there.
But my memories of the power of our love which was very rare

I believe in the spiritual world and hope you will give me a sign.
A sliver of faith that that we will reunite after a short time.
My love comes straight from the heart of your Snuggy Bear.
With knowledge that "JILL...JILL, I KNOW YOU ARE THERE!"

With love forever after,

Snuggy Bear

Love

Love is intangible, it's strong, its' an incredible feeling,
That starts with a commitment both emotional and revealing.

Love is hard, but beautiful, it bonds two souls that are best together.
It's inside your heart, it's passionate and last beyond forever.

Love is not part time; love is with you every minute of every day.
It's an extension of yourself and becomes you in every way.

You have been my love, right from the start
Now I'm lost and your death has broken my heart.

So how do I proceed when my world is turn upside-down?
Please tell me how I can survive if you are not around.

I am alone, I am afraid, and I miss you by my side.
Please God, give me the strength and be by guide.

My wish is that we rejoice and together we shine.
As our love will surpass this moment in time.

I love you,

John

Great Ride

I miss you in the morning
I miss you every day
I am hopeful I can find you
When it's time to find my way

Every night I think of you
And miss you in my heart
I pray you won't forget me
I hate when we're apart

I hope you'll look for me
As my end-game nears
I look forward to our meeting
So you can wipe away my tears

I love you beyond your death
I'm available any time
My work is done here on earth
And I'm well beyond my prime

Please show me the way
I'm hurt, alone and defeated
If I have things left undone
I will stay until completed

Hope to see you soon,
Love,
John

The Power Within

The day before yesterday I was young confident and ambitious.
The world was mine, as I was strong, smart and. adventurous.
But we learn that life is not always what it seems
And it can destroy your world, your life and your dreams.

Everything seems to be more complicated and gets harder
And we are forced to be more diligent and smarter.
We move through our life and learn to adapt.
Overcome our fears with our abilities yet untapped.

You possess the power to destroy fear even if unknown.
So don't be afraid to venture beyond your comfort zone.
You master your fears before they even begin.
Through the incredible power you possess within.

John Morgan Mullen

A Great Love Affair

You know how much I miss you.
Now that you have died.
So what do I do now?
That you are not by my side.

Life without you is hard
The unknown is full of fears
Anxiety about tomorrow's future
Is full of doubt and tears

I need just one more kiss,
Until our hearts beat as one.
So together we look back and smile
As we ride off into the sun.

Pretend you are with me.
We make such a great pair.
Let the light shine upon
Our Great Love Affair.

Love,

John Morgan Mullen

Beautiful Memories

Our past was filled with beautiful memories
Of our friends, our kids and our life of bliss.
We created a special world together,
I miss our life, our love and your kiss.

My memories of us will last forever,
In my mind, my body and in my heart.
The most incredible times of our journey
Were priceless, as our life was a work of art.

You were loved deep within my soul,
To guide me thru the emptiness and pain.
Please help me find my way,
To be strong so I can make it through the rain.

You left me empty the day you passed away
And I wish you peace, as we had great ride.
We became a force that filled our life with joy
And I dearly wish you were still by my side.

Love,

John

...Yesterday, Today & Tomorrow...
...It's your Past, your Present & your Future...

Yesterday was your "PAST"
It's your story etched in stone.
Your life's journey is unfolding.
And our Past we must own.

Today is your "PRESENT"
That provides you your chance.
To plan for your tomorrows,
To learn, enjoy, improve and enhance.

Tomorrow is your "FUTURE",
So develop your game plan.
Tomorrow leads to your forever,
And it's entirely in your hands.

John Morgan Mullen

Love Story

The first time I saw you,
You captured my heart.
A chance meeting at Michigan State
It was the perfect start.

The start of a Romance.
We were an incredible match.
You were my dream girl
And my Perfect Catch.

You were the love of my life,
Thru fun, success, pain and glory.
For fifty-five years as husband and wife.
We created the perfect "Love Story".

Love,

John

Change

Nanotechnology, stem cells research, robotic and autonomous cars,
DNA sequencing, liquid biopsy, 3-D printing and exploring the stars.
Our objective is to evaluate our technology for our future years.
To Increase our preparation and knowledge to eliminate fears.

The speed of change is mirrored by the speed of light,
Making today's artificial intelligence obsolete overnight.
New technologies are exciting, scary and a little strange.
So how do we adapt in our continuous world of change?

Alexa, Siri and Watson have helped put us in the fast lane.
With our new world of technology being our runaway train.
But change is our friend and presents opportunity at every turn.
And as always, the more you know the more you learn.

So crawl inside your head and examine your goals.
Your choices, education and passions all plays huge roles.
You must find your niche in those disciplines that will be hot.
As your future comes whether you are prepared or not.

The jobs of yesterday will cease to exist or will seriously decline.
Employment opportunities change, as our road is never a straight line.
Our road map and research provide us the certainty of knowing.
As it's easier to get there if you know where you're going.

John Morgan Mullen

Love is Forever

The contents of these vessel contain the love of my life.
It is my remembrance of Jill, my world, my partner and wife.
It's her physical ashes that I can hold close to my heart.
We can talk, laugh and cry until we are no longer apart.

We created our life together and now you are gone.
I miss you and am desperately trying to carry-on.
The contents of these containers allow me to hold you near.
And realize that Our Love is Forever as I shed a tear.
Until We Meet Again,

Love,

John

Dear God,

Your Shining Star

I have found your SHINING STAR.
You must be busy and have a lot to do.
But PLEASE GOD, look for Jill,
She's kind, sweet and beautiful too.

She would be a proud addition
To your INNER circle of SAINTS.
She would qualify with the highest
Quality and brightest of candidates.

She was kind, generous and loving
And my wife for fifty-five years
Qualifying her for immediate induction
Into Sainthood as she had very few peers.

Now you might say who this guy?
And who do you think you are?
You're right… but Jill is made for HEAVEN
And <u>she will be</u> YOUR SHINING STAR.

Morgan

Is the Game is Over?

We fought hard against Cancer's powerful breakout
Life is a Game were our time clock has run out

Cancer has a mind of its own and doesn't ask permission
It's aggressive, it's powerful, and loaded with ambition

It's strong, it attacks our cells before they can mend
Our destiny takes control and brought our lives to an end

But life doesn't stop as we take our last breath
As we a start of a new chapter called Life after Death

Throughout our life we have fought hard to win
But the Game isn't over as our New World begins

John Morgan Mullen

Myself

I am one with myself,
Independent, Unafraid & Strong.
I stand alone in my space,
Whether right or wrong.

My positions in my head
Describes my soul.
They define my why's,
As I attempt to achieve my goals.

I am compromised
With some of my views
Right, Wrong & in between
Some I win and some I lose

I must go on
I expand over time.
I change… I adjust
But I will be just fine

John Morgan Mullen

Alone

Depression is hard and it cut me to the bone.
I have support but am still all alone.

My friends love me and I know they care,
As I suffer thru my emptiness and despair.

With my loss of Jill, my life w/o her begins,
Just as <u>my</u> personal world is coming to an end.

The doctors concur I'm on a runaway train
As Cancer takes over in my life's final game.

John Morgan Mullen

Note from the Author

Dear Readers,

Poetry is an art that has taken a number of different avenues to present the Poet's creative thoughts. Poetry is an artistic, sophisticated and creative use of words that tell the Poets story. There are a number of poetry technique utilized to present a concise and condensed messages about everything from our world, our life and loves, as well as, our fears and joys.

"Straight From the Heart" is a collection of poems that I have compiled over the last several years that you hopefully will find enlightening, humoristic, entertaining and even romantic. The subject matter is everything from life and death, from love to hate, sickness and health, and success to failures. Many are directly related to my life and those close to me. With all of my poem being written…. "Straight From the Heart".

"To a child, LOVE is spelled T-I-M-E."

Helen, John, and Bill — Family Love

"Good Morning" at Our Michigan Home

Nancy, Pat, Jill, and John in Mexico

Jill and I at the start of our wonderful journey

Brother Bill, Sister Mary, and Helen

John and Jill the first year at MSU

Hailey — My Fishing Buddy

Bill, Helen, Jim, and John. Great Team.

Todd with coho salmon in Lake Michigan

Our dear Kappa sorority friends. Notice they all have a drink in their hands. Go Kappas!

Hailey, "I caught the most fish,"...Caitlyn, "Yeah, but I caught the biggest!"

Wow. To be young again.

John with hair.

John and Hailey fishing off the dock in Michigan.

Wow!

Jill with "Wind Song" her best friend

Todd and Jill

Jake and Jill

Love you!

Jill and John

MSU 1964

Jill

Stephanie and John. Good luck!

Boat trip in the Bahamas

A love affair between Jill and Wind Song.

Steph and Mike's wedding

Stephanie and John. Laughter is priceless.

Wow. I was a lucky guy.

Jake and John. These two are up to something.

Brennan, "Now is he gonna bite me?!"

Love Lasts Forever

Clark's, Burnard's & Mullen's family reunion in Michigan

Love

Joyce with her son Sean. "I couldn't be prouder."

The Jonasen's with Shirley and her kids in Honor of Lief. "God Bless America"

Jake's graduation from Univ of Illinois

Jake's graduating from University of Illinois

Best Friends Nancy & Pat Bollman

Sean and Jill

Jill and Abby

Sophie and Abbey "Best Friends Forever"

Todd and Daisy

Erik, Jenny, and Joyce

The Jonasen Girls Jill, Joyce, Shirley, and Jenny

Leif Omar Jonasen. The best dad ever!

Jill with her mom and her brothers and sisters.

Jenny, Ryan, and Shirley

Rick, Jenny, and Ryan

www.ingramcontent.com/pod-product-compliance
Lightning Source LLC
Chambersburg PA
CBHW061808070526
44586CB00024B/2759